Go Ahead EAT: I Dare You

Go Ahead EAT: I Dare You

Angie Lucarini

Printed in the United States of America

Publishing services by Selah Publishing Group, LLC, Indiana. The views expressed or implied in this work do not necessarily reflect those of Selah Publishing Group.

ISBN: 1-58930-152-8
Library of Congress Control Number: 2005903385

In loving Memory of My Precious Niece Priscilla L. Penque who went home to be with the Lord at the young age of 14 on July 11th 2004. She will be forever loved and missed.

Contents

Preface

Let's face it, no matter what their race, nationality, age, or denomination, people love to *eat.* I'm here to encourage you, even dare you to go ahead and *eat, eat, eat;* I guarantee the results will be life changing.

Now hold on a minute, put down those chips, don't be so quick to reach for that pint of chocolate ice cream; While it is a fact that we need to eat in order to nourish our bodies; the eating I'm referring to has nothing to do with our physical bodies. I'm talking about feeding our spiritual bodies.

If you are like most people, your spiritual bodies are in real need of a spiritual breakthrough. The kind mentioned in the bible. We are all praying for God to do that special something in our life. Like many, you may be crying out, "When God, when?" I want to help you to come up to a higher level in your walk of life, to receive all that God has for you, and to experience a little bit of heaven right here on earth. How do I propose to do that, you might ask.

One night as I lay sleeping with my 1 year old boy sprawled out across my stomach, God gave me a very simple and easy to remember concept. And so, at 3:00 in the morning, I reached over in the dark, grabbed a pen, and note pad, and jotted it down. My husband opened his eyes, looked at me like I was a lunatic, and asked "What are you doing?". I answered, "just writing".

Are You ready to begin your life-changing journey to reach your miracle? As you embark, keep in mind a saying I've heard so often before, *You can't keep doing the same thing and expect different results.* Having said that, put on your safety bib, and get ready to *eat, eat, eat.*

EAT is an acronym which is the basis for this book. Through-out the book, I will refer to it and discuss it, as it applies to scripture, and your life.

Expect Big
Ask specifically for your need
Thank God now

Chapter 1

Expect Big

Are you one of those people who think nothing good can ever happen to you? Do you not enter contests, because you know you'll never win? When you pray, do you hesitate to ask for anything at all, let alone anything seemingly impossible, since you know that God won't answer your prayer? If you answered yes to any of these questions, shame on you. If you answered yes to all of them, then you need serious help. The good news is that I'm here to give it to you.

To begin with, everyone has been or will be able to answer yes to one of the above questions at some point in their life. You are certainly not alone. Look at David for example (from the biblical story of David and Goliath, also the author of most of the book of psalms in the bible). At one point, God called David a man after his own heart. Yet, at another point in David's life (psalm 22:1) he cries out, "My God, My God why have you forsaken me?" At that time he didn't feel God's presence. Haven't we all been there? Surely if we feel that the Lord has abandoned us, then we would find it very difficult to believe that He would want to listen to us, answer our prayers, and furthermore desire to bless us big time.

Well, I'm here to tell you that not only does God promise <u>never</u> to leave us, nor forsake us, but in Ephesians 3:20 of the bible it says, "Now to Him who is *able to* do *exceedingly abundantly above* all that we ask or think, according to the power that works in us...." The truth is that God not only is absolutely able to do the impossible (Matthew 19:26), but He wants to. The bible tells us that He loves us more than anyone ever has or will. He created us. He is our Heavenly Father. As earthly parents we want nothing but the very best for our children, how much more our Lord who created us in the very image of His only begotten son wants the very best for us. Knowing that, we should go ahead and **EXPECT BIG**. Jabez did. Why not you? What have you got to lose? You've got everything to gain. Start expecting for exceedingly and abundantly more. Believe that God can and will do it for you. What is your need right now? Well, start professing it to be met right now. Romans 4:17 teaches us to speak those things that aren't as though they were. Speak it, believe it, and get ready to receive it. You deserve it!

Chapter 2

Ask Specifically for Your Need

The *A*, which is the second letter in the acronym *EAT*, stands for Ask Specifically For Your Need. When a child asks his/her parent for something, are they vague in their requests? The answer is no. Can you imagine children asking, "Mama, for my birthday will you buy me a toy?" or " Dad, after my baseball game could we go out for some food?" Instead, you would be much more likely to hear the child asking their parent for a specific type of toy (for example at my house it might be a Space Godzilla); or a certain type of food, heck most kids will even tell you where they want to go to eat it (an example might be to go for ice cream at Twist O Mist).

The point that I'm trying to make is that just as children wouldn't speak in general terms when asking their parents for something, we as children of the Most High should not do so in our prayers. God wants us to be specific in our prayers. The bible tells us that God knows the number of hairs on our head. Can you imagine that? If your hair is anything like mine, you know the kind that takes on a Jimmy Hendrix type of style once the humidity hits, then that's a huge feat. Furthermore, the scriptures say that He has our name written on the palm of His hand. Doesn't that tell you that our Lord cares for, and is concerned with <u>every</u> detail of our life? The book of Philippians gives us an outline, or a type of formula for specific prayer. In Philippians 4:6 it says "Don't worry about anything; instead, pray about everything; tell God your needs and don't forget to thank him for his answers."

So when you pray, be specific. Does this mean that if you are specific, God will give you everything you ask for? To that question, I would have to emphatically say no. As parents, do we say yes to everything that our children ask us for? Of course not. In the same way, God's answer to our prayers may sometimes be *NO*. Though we don't like that answer, we must trust that God will work all things together for good for those who love the Lord and are called according to his plans and purposes for our life, as stated in the bible (Romans 8:28).

I urge you to start asking specifically for your needs today. Begin with just a few major needs in your life, or in the lives of those you know. Write them down, then lift those up consistently before the Lord in prayer. As you receive the answers to your prayers, check them off, and journal just how God answered you and when. I assure you this alone will be life changing. Not only will it be great training grounds for facilitating you to become more persistent and specific in your prayers, but also it will minister to you and others again and again when facing the same or similar situations. We sometimes forget how God has previously worked miracles in our lives. It is in those times, when the going gets tough, and it will, those are the instances when we can go to our journal. It will quickly end our pity party, and get us back on the faith track. So go ahead, dig in, and begin eating your way to victory. As you do, you will soon start shedding those extra pounds. You know the heavy weight which burdens us in the form of low expectations, negativity, and hopelessness. Purpose it in your mind today to lose that excess baggage. You can do it!

Chapter 3

Thank God Now

The third, and final part of the acronym *EAT* represents THANK GOD NOW. We should not wait until we have everything we want, just the way we want it, until we have a thankful heart. If this is the case, and unfortunately it is with many, we will never be happy. Too often we miss out on the joys of life, because we can't take our eyes off of the voids of life. We then fail to see the blessings, which are right in front of us.

I remember a song I used to sing in church, where one of the verses reads, "with clapping hands and happy sounds, make a joyful noise unto the Lord". God wants us to be happy. He wants us to enjoy all that we have, while on the way to reaching our full potential. Picture if you will a child getting four of the six things she wanted for her birthday. Now imagine that child not enjoying, not playing with, barely even looking at those gifts, because all she can do is cry and complain about the two she didn't receive. How disappointing that would be to the parent who purchased the gifts with much love and hope for pleasing that child.

Does this sound familiar? It should. Though we hate to liken ourselves to the spoiled child presented in the above example, we are much like her. Don't we often fail to thank God for all that He has and is doing in our lives, all the while seeking more? I pose this thought, not to condemn you, but to enlighten you. The bible says, " in all things give thanks". It doesn't say to give thanks for all things, but in all things.

Take a really good look around. Like me, I'm sure you'll find that you have so much to give God thanks and praise for. While you are waiting for your miracle, give the Lord thanks for all that you have. I'm not just talking about verbal thanks, but a thankful heart and attitude as well. If you are thankful, you will not be grumbling and complaining all of the time. Instead, your thankful attitude will show in all you do. A thankful heart is a joyful heart. This type of atmosphere is contagious and inviting. Others will want to be around you more. Spending time with you will be a blessing to people.

Try giving the Lord thanks for the answers to your prayers that are already on the way. One of the names of God is Jehovah Jireh (which means the Lord will provide). God has already provided for all of our needs. Rest in knowing that He will take care of your needs. Begin to call your blessings in. As Romans 4:17 models, speak those things that aren't as though they were. Not only is speaking positive a heck of a lot healthier for you, than speaking and thinking negatively, but it will keep your heart and mind at peace and in an expectant mode. You will actually be putting your faith in God, as you prepare to receive your miracle. And you know what power there is in faith..... In Matthew 11:23, it actually tells us that faith can move mountains. Friends, if God can separate seas, raise people from the dead, walk on water, make winds and storms stop at His command, then surely He is able to meet our greatest and smallest needs. Begin to trust God now. Expect Big, Ask God Specifically For Your Need, and Thank God Now. Well, what are you waiting for? EAT up! Bon Appetit!

Whistle

Now that you are ready to *EAT* up, I want you to do something else for me. I want you to whistle. God gave me a very simple, yet precise word to share with you. He said, "Angie, I want you to *Whistle While you Wait.*" Similar to the old song, "Whistle while you work", God wants us to whistle while we await our miracle. Now this may sound silly, even unorthodox, but it is a very important breakthrough, which you need to grab a hold of on your way to victory.

How sad it is when people wait, and wait, and wait for the answers to their prayers to come, and they do so miserably, kicking and screaming all the way. Upon getting ready to drive across country for a vacation to Florida, a man prayed asking God to bless his trip. He asked that this be the most exciting, invigorating, eye-opening trip ever. Well, as he and his wife drove to Florida the gentleman complained the whole time about everything from traffic and expenses, to the length of time it took to get there. Once they reached their destination, they settled in for the night.

The man threw himself on the hotel room bed and said, "That was the worst trip ever. Finally, we're here". A few moments later, his wife joined him on the bed. After getting comfortable under the warm blanket, she smiled, and prayed, "Thank you so much Lord for a wonderful, safe trip, and for all of the breathtaking scenes of nature we saw along the way. I know that was only the beginning, but boy what an intro Lord. I can't wait to see what the rest of the trip holds..." Here we have two people going in the same direction, hoping for the same outcome, the only difference is, she was whistling while she waited.

We should all take a lesson from that woman. I often tell my friends to pinch their cheeks, jump up and down, dance, sing, do what you need to, in order to stir yourself up. While you Expect Big, Ask God Specifically For Your Need, and Thank God Now, start whistling while you wait. Enjoy every minute on the way to receiving your miracle. Not only will you enjoy life more if you do, but you will be more open to hearing and learning from God along the way. Some people not only waste precious time being miserable, while they are waiting on God, or going through one of the many storms of life; but they also may miss the very thing they've been praying for, due to their eyes being closed with bitterness and hurt. God wants us to be an active participant in our waiting.

Please, don't waste another minute of your precious life. Go on, get up and start whistling. Hey, if nothing else, it will make you laugh and smile. Isn't that a great place to be? Happy people are healthier people. Well, what are you waiting for? **Go Ahead EAT I Dare You!** Then, begin to *Whistle While You Wait.* I promise it won't hurt, and you won't gain a pound!

Afterthoughts

Mountains Turned Miracles

Once again, as is usually the case with me, a song comes to my mind, "Ain't no Mountain High Enough". Being a teacher, I can't help but to tell my oldest of three boys that "ain't" is not proper English. However at this time, there seems to be no word more fitting. For truly as it applies to God, there "ain't no mountain high enough" to keep God from turning it into a miracle of living water. Below are just a few of the many times where I've seen evidence of this in my own life.

MOM

Over ten years ago, I was awakened from my sleep to hear gut wrenching screams of horror. I was still living with my parents at the time. After realizing that I was not dreaming, I went downstairs to find my father crying over my mother's lifeless body. She lay in a pool of blood. A few feet away, was a bathtub full of blood. My Dad was trying to revive her. Soon came the blur of firefighters and sirens to carry my Mom out on a stretcher.

In shock, I went to my room. All I could do was pray that she not die. I asked for a miracle. Then, as if I was a broken record, I proceeded to repeat the Lord's Prayer over and over again until almost an hour later when the phone call came. It was the hospital. My Mother had a fibroid tumor the size of a grapefruit in one of her ovaries. It exploded. The doctor said that with the amount of blood she lost, it was a miracle that she was alive.

A FRIEND

Many, many years ago while at a party, I watched someone who thought she was invincible, (you know the "Are you talking to me?" type of attitude) drop to the ground. She came down fast and hard, like a ton of bricks. She had accidentally overdosed on drugs. Due to fear, everyone present scattered, leaving her body, which had now gone into convulsions on the floor.

Besides one other onlooker who stood frozen and motionless, I was the only one who hadn't run. All I could do was pray as I watched her lips turn blue, and then her breathing stopped as she lay perfectly still. I then felt for a pulse. There was none. All the while, I kept praying Lord please help me, please don't let her die, and once again, I repeated the Lord's prayer as I began the process of mouth to mouth resuscitation. Within a few moments that felt more like a lifetime, she started coughing and vomiting. By then, the onlooker had left. I stayed with her for a couple of hours, pouring water on her shaking sweating body, offering her whatever comfort I could, all the while still praying in my head. She hadn't spoken anything audible for some time. When she did, she asked "did I die?" I said, "I believe so". She responded, "you saved my life". "No" I said, "God did".

MY MARRIAGE

Before my husband and I ever considered dating, God gave me a vision one night while I was praying. It was just as clear as if I had seen a movie screen in front of my face. It was of us at the altar getting married. I heard loud and clear from God that we would marry. I never told my husband until well after we began dating, and he told me that he loved me, and wanted to marry me.

After getting engaged several months later, we called off the engagement twice. I then decided to *let go and let God*. For two months we had no contact. By all outward appearances, and according to all the "talk of the town", we were through. This was one of the hardest times of our lives. It was painstaking to know that Ron was hurting so much, and yet to purposefully stay away, so as not to get in God's way. The only thing I could do was......(you guessed it) PRAY, PRAY, PRAY. After two long months, we saw each other one day. That same week, Ron showed up on my doorstep several times. A couple weeks later we were married. Three children later, here we are to tell about it.

RAPHAEL

While pregnant with my second of three sons, I was given the negative report that according to some prenatal tests, my child would very likely have birth defects or disease. My husband and I told no one about it. Instead, we made a decision to *EAT (Expect Big, Ask God specifically for our need, and Thank God now)*.

During that time, God spoke to us in unimaginable ways, letting us know that our son was healed, via television, the bible, and a prophet who knew nothing of our situation. On May 9th, 2002 our son Raphael (whose name means God has healed) was born healthy and precious as can be.

Miracles or mere coincidences? For me there is *NO DOUBT*. God took these mountains and turned them into miracles of living water. As **Joshua 24:15** says, "As for me and my family, we shall serve the Lord."

Afterthoughts: Mountains Turned Miracles

Well, what do you say? Are you hungry for a miracle? I pray that Jesus will take every one of your seemingly impossible mountains, and turn them into miracles of living water (Breathing, living, proof of God's Grace, Mercy, and Love). He most certainly is able! As you can see, He did it for me, and Romans 2:11 says that God is no respecter of persons. That means what He did for me, He can do for you.

Note From the Author

I am married to a wonderful, Godly man. We have three small boys. I hold a Bachelor's Degree in Elementary Education and a Master's Degree in Educational Foundations. I have completed my Permanent Certification. After teaching for nine years, I have chosen to be a stay-home mother while my children are small.

In addition to leading several co-ed bible studies over the past six years, and team teaching church school to high school children, my husband and I also served as leaders of a Couples' Ministry at our church for two years. I've appeared on a television show called "Women of Destiny" three times, and held a couple of Women's Conferences, where I ministered the word of God to women of all ages. I currently hold a women's bible study in my home. We meet every other week to study the word of God, pray for and encourage one another, and share testimonies of what the Lord is doing in our lives. Most recently, I have completed a book titled, *"Maximize Your Marriage in 21 Days"*. Both my husband and I come from large families. We treasure the love and support that comes from them.

Having listed all my credentials that look so good on paper, it is essential that I say this. Neither my husband nor I would be who we are today, nor have the marriage and family we do today, if it weren't for our relationships with Jesus Christ. It is in Christ that we have truly been blessed, and have begun to *live*, striving to be the best that we can be. All of those other things are really nothing, without Him. If you were blessed by this book, I only pray that you will buy a copy for a friend, that they too may be blessed.

To order additional copies of

Go Ahead EAT: I Dare You

have your credit card ready and call
1 800-917-BOOK (2665)

or e-mail
orders@selahbooks.com

or order online at
www.selahbooks.com